CHILE UNVEILED

THE ULTIMATE TRAVEL COMPANION

HUDSON MYRON

TABLE OF CONTENTS

WELCOME TO CHILE

Welcome to Chile, a land of contrasts, where the arid expanse of the Atacama Desert meets the icy embrace of Patagonia's glaciers, and where the vibrant energy of Santiago merges with the serene beauty of Easter Island. As you step onto Chilean soil, you embark on a journey of discovery—one that will take you through breathtaking landscapes, rich cultural heritage, and unforgettable experiences.

Stretching over 4,300 kilometers (2,670 miles) along the western coast of South America, Chile is a country of unparalleled geographical diversity. To the north, the Atacama Desert, often referred to as the driest place on Earth, captivates with its stark beauty—endless salt flats, otherworldly rock formations, and skies that shimmer with a million stars. Here, in this seemingly inhospitable terrain, you'll discover unexpected oases teeming with life, and ancient petroglyphs that speak of civilizations long gone.

Venture southward, and you'll find yourself amidst the fertile valleys and rolling vineyards of Chile's central region. This is where the heart of Chilean wine country beats, producing some of the finest varietals in the world. Immerse yourself in the rich aromas and flavors of Chilean wine as you tour the historic vineyards of the

Colchagua Valley, or sip a glass of crisp Sauvignon Blanc overlooking the Pacific Ocean in the Casablanca Valley.

Further south lies Patagonia, a land of untamed beauty and raw wilderness. Here, jagged peaks pierce the sky, glaciers cascade into emerald lakes, and pristine forests teem with wildlife. Trek through the rugged terrain of Torres del Paine National Park, where guanacos roam freely and condors soar overhead. Or embark on a cruise through the icy waters of the Chilean fjords, where towering icebergs and majestic whales await at every turn.

But Chile's allure extends beyond its natural wonders—it is also a country rich in history, culture, and tradition. In the colorful streets of Valparaíso, a UNESCO World Heritage Site, you'll find a city alive with creativity and artistic expression, where vibrant murals adorn every corner and lively street performers entertain passersby. In the remote reaches of Easter Island, you'll encounter the enigmatic Moai statues, silent sentinels of a bygone era, standing watch over a land steeped in mystery and legend.

As you journey through Chile, you'll be embraced by the warmth and hospitality of its people, whose resilience and spirit are as enduring as the landscapes that surround them. Whether you're savoring the flavors of traditional

Chilean cuisine, exploring the ancient ruins of indigenous civilizations, or simply soaking in the breathtaking beauty of the natural world, Chile promises to be a journey like no other—a tapestry of experiences that will leave an indelible mark on your soul.

So, welcome to Chile—where adventure beckons at every turn, and the spirit of exploration knows no bounds. Whether you're scaling towering peaks, delving into ancient cultures, or simply basking in the tranquility of nature, you're sure to find something to inspire and delight in this remarkable land. So come, embark on this journey of discovery, and let Chile unveil its wonders to you in all their splendor. Welcome to Chile—where the adventure of a lifetime awaits.

CONCÓN

CHAPTER ONE
PLANNING YOUR JOURNEY

Embarking on a journey to Chile is an exciting endeavor, but careful planning is essential to ensure a smooth and memorable experience. In this chapter, we provide invaluable insights into the practical aspects of planning your trip, from understanding visa requirements and essential travel documents to choosing the best time to visit this diverse country. Navigating Chile's extensive transportation network can be daunting, but fear not—we offer expert advice on getting around, whether you're exploring the bustling streets of Santiago or venturing into the remote corners of Patagonia.

In addition to logistical considerations, we delve into the cultural nuances and local customs that will enrich your journey and help you connect with the heart and soul of Chile. From language tips for travelers to safety advice and common scams to avoid, our comprehensive guide equips you with the knowledge and confidence to navigate Chile with ease. Whether you're a first-time visitor or a seasoned traveler, our chapter on planning your journey lays the groundwork for an unforgettable adventure in this captivating land.

VISA REQUIREMENTS AND TRAVEL DOCUMENTS

Navigating the visa requirements and gathering the necessary travel documents is a crucial step in planning your journey to Chile. Fortunately, for many travelers, the process is relatively straightforward. Citizens of over 90 countries, including the United States, Canada, Australia, and most European nations, do not require a visa to enter Chile for tourism purposes if their stay is less than 90 days. However, it's essential to check the latest visa regulations specific to your nationality, as requirements can vary.

For those who do require a visa, the process typically involves submitting an application to the nearest Chilean consulate or embassy. Depending on your circumstances, you may need to provide supporting documents such as proof of accommodation, a return ticket, and evidence of sufficient funds to cover your stay. Processing times can vary, so it's advisable to apply well in advance of your planned travel dates.

In addition to obtaining a visa, all travelers to Chile must have a valid passport with at least six months' validity beyond the intended period of stay. Upon arrival, immigration officials will stamp your passport, indicating the duration of your authorized stay. It's essential to keep your passport safe throughout your trip, as you'll need it for hotel check-ins, internal flights, and various other administrative purposes. Additionally, travelers should carry a printed or digital copy of their travel itinerary, including accommodation reservations, transportation details, and emergency contacts, to facilitate smooth entry into Chile and ensure a hassle-free travel experience. By staying informed about visa requirements and ensuring you have the necessary travel documents in order, you can set off on your Chilean adventure with confidence and peace of mind.

SALTOS DEL PETROHUE

BEST TIME TO VISIT CHILE

Determining the optimal time to visit Chile depends largely on your travel preferences and the regions you plan to explore, as this diverse country experiences varied climates and weather patterns throughout the year. To make the most of your Chilean adventure, it's essential to consider the unique characteristics of each season and how they align with your interests and desired experiences.

1. **Spring (September to November):** As the country emerges from the chill of winter, spring brings vibrant blooms, mild temperatures, and longer daylight hours, making it an ideal time to explore Chile's natural wonders. Patagonia comes to life with lush greenery, and the Atacama Desert bursts into bloom with colorful wildflowers. Spring also marks the beginning of the tourist season in many parts of the country, so expect larger crowds and higher prices, especially in popular destinations like Torres del Paine National Park and Easter Island.

2. **Summer (December to February):** For sun-seekers and outdoor enthusiasts, Chile's summer offers endless opportunities for adventure. With warm temperatures and clear skies, this is the perfect time to explore the country's coastal beaches, hike in the Andean foothills, and embark on wildlife-spotting

excursions. Patagonia experiences its peak tourist season during the summer months, with long daylight hours and milder temperatures making it an ideal time for trekking and outdoor activities. However, be prepared for higher prices and crowded attractions, especially in popular tourist areas.

3. **Autumn (March to May):** As temperatures begin to cool and crowds thin out, autumn presents a quieter and more tranquil side of Chile. The country's vineyards come alive with the vibrant hues of fall foliage, offering a picturesque backdrop for wine tasting tours and leisurely countryside drives. In Patagonia, the landscapes are ablaze with fiery reds and oranges, creating a stunning contrast against the snow-capped peaks. Autumn is also an excellent time for cultural exploration, with festivals and events celebrating Chilean traditions and harvest season.

4. **Winter (June to August):** While Chile's winter may not be as harsh as in some other parts of the world, it does bring cooler temperatures and occasional rainfall, particularly in central and southern regions. For snow enthusiasts, this is the prime time to hit the slopes in the Andes, with world-class ski resorts like Valle Nevado and Portillo offering excellent conditions for skiing and snowboarding. In the northern desert regions, winter

brings cooler, more comfortable temperatures for exploring attractions like the Atacama Desert and Elqui Valley. Additionally, winter is an excellent time for wildlife viewing in Patagonia, with fewer tourists and the chance to spot iconic species such as penguins and whales.

Ultimately, the best time to visit Chile depends on your interests, budget, and tolerance for crowds and weather conditions. Whether you're seeking sun-drenched beaches, high-altitude adventures, or cultural immersion, Chile offers something for every traveler, year-round. By carefully planning your visit based on the seasonal highlights and your personal preferences, you can ensure a truly unforgettable experience in this captivating country.

TRANSPORTATION OPTIONS AND GETTING AROUND

Chile, with its diverse landscapes spanning from the Atacama Desert in the north to the fjords of Patagonia in the south, offers travelers a wealth of experiences to explore. As you embark on your journey through this captivating country, navigating its vast expanse becomes a key consideration. With a multitude of transportation options available, from bustling cities to remote wilderness areas, understanding how to get around Chile efficiently and safely is essential for an unforgettable adventure.

1. **Air Travel:** Chile's main entry point for international travelers is Santiago's Comodoro Arturo Merino Benítez International Airport, which offers connections to major cities worldwide. Domestic flights within Chile are operated by several airlines, including LATAM Airlines, Sky Airline, and JetSMART, providing convenient access to destinations across the country. Whether you're flying to the northern deserts, the central wine regions, or the southern fjords, domestic air travel offers a quick and efficient way to cover large distances.

2. **Long-Distance Buses:** For travelers seeking a more budget-friendly and scenic option, Chile's extensive

network of long-distance buses provides an excellent alternative. Companies like Turbus, Pullman Bus, and Cruz del Sur operate comfortable coaches with amenities such as reclining seats, onboard restrooms, and Wi-Fi, making long journeys more comfortable. Overnight buses are particularly popular for routes covering substantial distances, allowing travelers to save on accommodation costs while maximizing their time for exploration.

3. **Public Transportation in Cities:** In Chile's urban centers, including Santiago, Valparaíso, and Concepción, public transportation systems are efficient and well-developed. Santiago boasts an extensive metro network, complemented by an integrated bus system, providing convenient access to key attractions and neighborhoods. In Valparaíso, a UNESCO World Heritage Site, colorful trolleybuses and historic funiculars traverse the city's hilly terrain, offering scenic views of the Pacific Ocean. Taxis and ride-sharing services like Uber and Cabify are readily available in most cities, providing additional flexibility for getting around.

4. **Rental Cars and Camper Vans:** For travelers seeking independence and flexibility, renting a car or camper van offers the freedom to explore Chile at your own pace. Rental agencies are available at

major airports and cities, offering a range of vehicles to suit different budgets and preferences. Chile's well-maintained highways and roads provide scenic routes through breathtaking landscapes, from the coastal highways of the Atacama Desert to the winding mountain roads of Patagonia. However, travelers should exercise caution, especially in rural areas where road conditions may vary, and GPS coverage may be limited.

5. **Guided Tours and Adventure Excursions:** For those looking for curated experiences and expert guidance, guided tours and adventure excursions offer immersive ways to explore Chile's diverse landscapes and attractions. Whether hiking in Torres del Paine National Park, embarking on a wine tasting tour in the Colchagua Valley, or exploring the lunar landscapes of the Atacama Desert, guided tours provide opportunities to learn from knowledgeable local guides and connect with fellow travelers. These tours cater to a variety of interests and activity levels, ensuring that there's something for everyone to enjoy.

6. **Ferries and Boats:** Chile's extensive coastline and numerous lakes offer opportunities for travel by ferry and boat. In the south, ferries connect mainland Chile with the archipelagos of Chiloé and Tierra del Fuego, providing access to remote

communities and pristine wilderness areas. Travelers can embark on multi-day cruises through the fjords of Patagonia, where towering glaciers and abundant wildlife await. Additionally, scenic boat tours are available on many of Chile's picturesque lakes, including Lake Llanquihue and Lake Pehoé, offering a unique perspective of the surrounding landscapes.

7. **Cycling and Walking:** For eco-conscious travelers and outdoor enthusiasts, cycling and walking offer sustainable and immersive ways to explore Chile's natural beauty. Many cities, including Santiago and Valparaíso, have dedicated bike lanes and pedestrian-friendly promenades, making it easy to navigate urban areas on two wheels or on foot. In rural areas, cycling tours and hiking trails provide opportunities to explore scenic countryside, from rolling vineyards to rugged coastlines. Popular routes include the Carretera Austral in Patagonia and the Lake District's Circuito de los Lagos, offering breathtaking views and unforgettable experiences along the way.

8. **Regional Trains:** While Chile's railway network is not as extensive as those in other countries, there are still opportunities for train travel in certain regions. The TerraSur train operates between Santiago and Chillán, passing through the picturesque Maule

Valley and offering panoramic views of the countryside. In the Lake District, the Southern Railway connects the towns of Temuco and Victoria, providing a scenic journey through lush forests and fertile farmland. While train travel may be limited compared to other transportation options, it offers a leisurely and nostalgic way to experience Chile's landscapes and culture.

9. **Domestic Flights to Remote Destinations:** For travelers seeking to explore Chile's more remote and inaccessible regions, domestic flights to remote airstrips and airports provide convenient access. Charter flights and small aircraft operate routes to destinations such as Robinson Crusoe Island in the Juan Fernández Archipelago and the remote villages of the Aysén region in southern Patagonia. These flights offer a unique opportunity to discover isolated communities, pristine wilderness areas, and hidden gems off the beaten path.

Ultimately, the best way to navigate Chile depends on your travel preferences, itinerary, and budget. Many travelers opt for a combination of transportation modes to maximize flexibility and convenience. For example, you may choose to fly between major cities and regions, then rent a car or camper van for exploring more remote areas. Alternatively, guided tours and adventure excursions provide curated experiences with transportation included, allowing you to sit back, relax, and enjoy the journey while expert guides take care of the logistics. By considering the various transportation options available and planning your journey accordingly, you can create a customized itinerary that suits your travel style and ensures an unforgettable adventure through the diverse landscapes of Chile.

VOLCÁN PARINACOTA

CHAPTER TWO
INSIDER'S INSIGHTS

Gain a deeper understanding of Chile's rich culture and heritage with our insider's insights. In this chapter, we delve into the cultural nuances, local customs, and insider tips that will enhance your travel experience and allow you to connect more intimately with the heart and soul of Chile. From language tips for travelers to safety advice and common scams to avoid, we provide invaluable knowledge to help you navigate Chile with confidence and respect.

Discover the warmth and hospitality of the Chilean people as we uncover the hidden gems and off-the-beaten-path destinations that truly showcase the country's authenticity. Whether you're savoring traditional dishes in a local market, joining in on a lively street parade, or immersing yourself in the rhythms of Chilean music and dance, our insider's insights will ensure that you make the most of your time in this captivating land. With our expert guidance, you'll unlock the secrets of Chile and create memories that will last a lifetime.

CULTURAL ETIQUETTE AND CUSTOMS

Understanding the cultural etiquette and customs of Chile is essential for travelers looking to immerse themselves fully in the local way of life and to ensure respectful interactions with the people of Chile. With its rich blend of indigenous traditions, Spanish influences, and modern cosmopolitanism, Chilean culture is both diverse and dynamic, offering travelers a fascinating tapestry of customs to explore.

1. **Greetings and Social Interaction:** In Chilean culture, personal relationships and connections are highly valued, and greetings often involve physical contact such as hugs or kisses on the cheek. When meeting someone for the first time, a handshake is appropriate, followed by a kiss on the cheek if the relationship becomes more familiar. It's essential to greet everyone individually, starting with the oldest or most senior person present. Chileans are known for their warmth and hospitality, so expect to engage in friendly conversation and small talk, particularly in social settings.

2. **Respect for Elders and Authority:** Respect for elders and authority figures is deeply ingrained in Chilean culture, and it's essential to show deference and politeness in interactions with older individuals

or those in positions of power. This includes using formal titles such as "Señor" (Mr.) or "Señora" (Mrs.) when addressing older adults, and "Don" or "Doña" followed by their first name for added respect. It's also customary to stand when someone older or of higher status enters the room and to yield seats to them as a sign of deference and respect.

3. **Dining Etiquette:** Chilean cuisine is a reflection of the country's diverse geography and cultural heritage, and dining plays a central role in Chilean social life. When dining with Chileans, it's essential to observe proper etiquette, such as waiting for the host to begin eating before starting your meal and keeping your hands visible on the table. It's considered polite to try a bit of everything offered, even if it's unfamiliar, and to express appreciation for the meal with phrases like "Buen provecho" (Enjoy your meal) or "Está muy rico" (It's delicious). Additionally, it's customary to offer to help with the dishes or clean up after the meal as a gesture of gratitude to the host.

4. **Language and Communication:** Spanish is the official language of Chile, and while many Chileans speak English, particularly in urban areas and tourist destinations, it's always appreciated to make an effort to communicate in Spanish. Learning a few basic phrases and greetings can go a long way in

building rapport and showing respect for Chilean culture. Additionally, Chilean Spanish has its unique slang and expressions, so be prepared for some linguistic surprises and don't be afraid to ask for clarification if needed.

As a visitor to Chile, it's essential to be culturally sensitive and respectful of local customs and traditions. Avoid discussing sensitive topics such as politics, religion, or the country's history, particularly during social gatherings, unless invited to do so by your Chilean hosts. It's also important to be mindful of personal space and to refrain from intrusive questions or behaviors that may be considered rude or offensive. By demonstrating cultural sensitivity and respect for Chilean customs, you'll foster positive relationships and create memorable experiences during your time in this vibrant and welcoming country.

LANGUAGE TIPS FOR TRAVELERS

Navigating Chile's vibrant culture and engaging with its warm-hearted people can be greatly enhanced by learning a few key language tips. While Spanish is the official language of Chile, understanding the nuances of Chilean Spanish and incorporating basic phrases into your interactions can go a long way in fostering meaningful connections and making your travel experience more enriching.

1. **Learn Basic Spanish Phrases:** Even if you're not fluent in Spanish, learning a few basic phrases can significantly improve your communication skills and make interactions smoother. Start with essentials such as greetings ("Hola" for hello, "Buenos días" for good morning, "Buenas tardes" for good afternoon, and "Buenas noches" for good evening), polite phrases ("Por favor" for please and "Gracias" for thank you), and common expressions ("Disculpe" for excuse me and "Perdón" for pardon me).

2. **Practice Pronunciation:** Chilean Spanish has its unique accent and pronunciation, so practicing the way words are pronounced can help you better understand and be understood by locals. Pay attention to the pronunciation of vowels, consonants, and accent marks, as they can change the meaning of

words. Don't be afraid to ask for clarification or repetition if you're unsure about something, as Chileans are generally patient and understanding with language learners.

3. **Use Chilean Slang and Expressions:** Chilean Spanish is peppered with slang words and expressions that may differ from standard Spanish. Familiarize yourself with common Chilean slang terms ("weón" for dude or buddy, "poh" for an emphasis or affirmation, and "cachai" for you know or understand) to better connect with locals and add authenticity to your conversations. While slang can be fun and informal, use it appropriately and be mindful of the context to avoid any misunderstandings.

4. **Be Patient and Open-Minded:** Learning a new language can be challenging, but don't be discouraged by mistakes or misunderstandings. Approach language learning with a sense of curiosity and openness, and embrace opportunities to practice and improve your skills. Be patient with yourself and others, and don't hesitate to use gestures, facial expressions, or visual aids to aid communication when necessary.

5. **Seek Language Learning Opportunities:** Take advantage of language learning opportunities during your travels in Chile, whether through formal

classes, language exchange meetups, or interactions with locals. Practice speaking Spanish whenever you can, whether ordering food at a restaurant, shopping at a market, or asking for directions on the street. Many Chileans will appreciate your efforts to speak their language and may even offer encouragement or corrections to help you improve.

By incorporating these language tips into your travel toolkit, you'll not only enhance your ability to communicate effectively in Chile but also deepen your cultural understanding and appreciation of this diverse and welcoming country. Language is a bridge that connects people across borders and cultures, and by embracing the Spanish language during your travels in Chile, you'll forge meaningful connections and create lasting memories along the way.

SAFETY TIPS AND COMMON SCAMS TO AVOID

Ensuring your safety while traveling in Chile is paramount to enjoying a worry-free and memorable experience. While Chile is generally considered safe for tourists, it's essential to be aware of potential risks and take precautions to protect yourself and your belongings. By staying informed and exercising vigilance, you can minimize the likelihood of encountering safety issues and focus on enjoying all that Chile has to offer.

1. **Stay Aware of Your Surroundings:** Maintaining awareness of your surroundings is one of the most effective ways to stay safe while traveling in Chile. Pay attention to your surroundings, particularly in crowded areas or tourist hotspots where pickpockets and petty thieves may operate. Keep your belongings close to you at all times, and avoid displaying valuables such as expensive jewelry, cameras, or smartphones in public.

2. **Use Reliable Transportation:** When moving around Chile, opt for reputable transportation options such as licensed taxis, ridesharing services like Uber or Cabify, or official public transportation. Avoid accepting rides from unmarked or unofficial vehicles, particularly late at night or in unfamiliar areas. If using public transportation, keep an eye on

your belongings and be cautious of crowded buses or metro trains where thefts may occur.

3. **Secure Your Accommodation:** Choose accommodations that prioritize safety and security, such as reputable hotels, hostels, or guesthouses with positive reviews and reliable security measures in place. When checking into your room, ensure that windows and doors are properly locked, and use hotel safes or secure lockers to store valuables when not in use. Familiarize yourself with emergency procedures and contact information for local authorities or emergency services in case of any unexpected incidents.

4. **Be Cautious of Scams:** Like any popular tourist destination, Chile is not immune to scams and fraudulent schemes aimed at unsuspecting travelers. Common scams to be aware of include distraction techniques, such as someone bumping into you or asking for directions while an accomplice steals your belongings, or overcharging for goods or services, particularly in tourist areas. Be cautious when approached by strangers offering unsolicited assistance or deals that seem too good to be true, and trust your instincts if something feels suspicious.

5. **Research Local Laws and Customs:** Before traveling to Chile, familiarize yourself with local laws, customs, and cultural norms to avoid

inadvertently offending or violating local regulations. Respect cultural traditions and customs, such as dressing modestly in religious sites or avoiding public displays of affection in conservative areas. Be aware of any restrictions or regulations regarding photography, particularly in sensitive or sacred locations.

By following these safety tips and remaining vigilant throughout your travels in Chile, you can minimize risks and enjoy a safe and rewarding experience exploring this beautiful and diverse country. Remember to trust your instincts, stay informed, and take precautions to protect yourself and your belongings, allowing you to focus on creating unforgettable memories and experiences during your time in Chile.

TORRES DE PAINE NATIONAL PARK

CHAPTER THREE
MUST-SEE STUNNING ATTRACTIONS

Prepare to be mesmerized by Chile's breathtaking natural wonders and awe-inspiring landscapes in this chapter dedicated to must-see stunning attractions. From the otherworldly beauty of the Atacama Desert to the majestic peaks of Torres del Paine National Park, Chile offers a diverse array of sights that will leave you speechless and longing for more.

Embark on a journey to the Atacama Desert, the driest desert in the world, where salt flats shimmer in the sun, geysers spout steam into the air, and lunar-like landscapes stretch as far as the eye can see. Explore the otherworldly Valle de la Luna (Valley of the Moon), where towering sand dunes, sculpted rock formations, and vibrant hues of red and orange create a surreal lunar landscape that's truly out of this world. For stargazers, the Atacama Desert boasts some of the clearest and darkest skies on Earth, offering unparalleled opportunities for stargazing and celestial observation that will leave you in awe of the universe's beauty.

Chile, a land of extraordinary diversity and natural beauty, boasts an array of stunning attractions that will leave travelers in awe of the planet's majestic landscapes. From the otherworldly deserts of the north to the pristine wilderness of Patagonia in the south, Chile offers a treasure trove of must-see sights that are sure to captivate the imagination and inspire a sense of wonder.

1. **Torres del Paine National Park:** Located in the southern reaches of Chilean Patagonia, Torres del Paine National Park is a Biosphere Reserve renowned for its dramatic peaks, sparkling lakes, and rugged beauty. The park's iconic granite spires, known as the Torres del Paine, dominate the skyline and provide a breathtaking backdrop for hiking, wildlife spotting, and photography. Visitors can explore a network of well-marked trails that lead through pristine forests, past shimmering glaciers, and along turquoise lakes, offering opportunities to encounter iconic Patagonian wildlife such as guanacos, foxes, and Andean condors. Whether trekking the renowned W Circuit or embarking on a day hike to the base of the towers, Torres del Paine National Park promises unforgettable adventures in one of the world's most stunning natural landscapes.

2. **Atacama Desert:** Venture to the northern reaches of Chile and discover the otherworldly beauty of the Atacama Desert, the driest desert on Earth. Here, vast salt flats, towering sand dunes, and surreal rock formations create a landscape that resembles a Martian moonscape. Highlights of the Atacama

Desert include the Valle de la Luna (Valley of the Moon), where wind-carved canyons and lunar-like landscapes stretch as far as the eye can see, and the otherworldly salt flats of the Salar de Atacama, home to flamingos, llamas, and other hardy desert species. Visitors can also marvel at the El Tatio Geysers, a field of steaming geothermal vents set against a backdrop of snow-capped volcanoes, or journey to the remote desert town of San Pedro de Atacama, where ancient ruins and indigenous cultures add depth and intrigue to this surreal desert landscape.

3. **Easter Island (Rapa Nui):** Situated in the southeastern Pacific Ocean, Easter Island, or Rapa Nui as it is known to its indigenous inhabitants, is one of the most remote inhabited islands on Earth. Famous for its enigmatic moai statues, towering stone monoliths carved by the island's ancient Polynesian inhabitants, Easter Island offers a glimpse into a fascinating and mysterious past. Visitors can explore the island's archaeological sites, including the iconic Ahu Tongariki, where 15 massive moai stand sentinel against the horizon, or hike to the rim of the volcanic crater at Rano Kau for panoramic views of the island and the Pacific Ocean beyond. With its rugged coastline, pristine beaches, and rich cultural heritage, Easter Island is a

must-visit destination for travelers seeking adventure, discovery, and a sense of wonder in one of the world's most remote and captivating locales.

4. **Chilean Fjords and Glaciers:** Embark on a voyage through the pristine wilderness of Chile's southern fjords and glaciers, where towering peaks, emerald forests, and sparkling waterways create a landscape of unparalleled beauty and grandeur. Cruise through the narrow channels and sheltered bays of the Chilean fjords, where snow-capped mountains plunge into the sea, and hidden waterfalls cascade down sheer cliffs. Marvel at the stunning beauty of glaciers such as the San Rafael Glacier, a towering wall of ice that calves into the tranquil waters of Laguna San Rafael, or the Pio XI Glacier, the largest glacier in South America. Along the way, keep an eye out for abundant wildlife, including seals, dolphins, and whales, as well as seabirds such as albatrosses, petrels, and penguins that call these remote and pristine waters home. Whether exploring by cruise ship, kayak, or small boat, the Chilean fjords and glaciers offer a once-in-a-lifetime opportunity to experience the raw beauty and untamed wilderness of one of the world's last great frontiers.

5. **Chiloé Archipelago:** Immerse yourself in the rich culture and natural beauty of the Chiloé

Archipelago, a cluster of islands located off the coast of southern Chile. Known for its distinctive wooden churches, traditional palafitos (stilt houses), and vibrant folklore, Chiloé offers a unique blend of indigenous and Spanish colonial influences that make it unlike anywhere else in Chile. Explore the island's charming towns and villages, such as Castro and Ancud, where colorful buildings line the waterfront and traditional handicrafts abound. Discover the island's natural wonders, including pristine beaches, lush forests, and tranquil lagoons teeming with birdlife. And don't miss the chance to sample Chiloé's famed cuisine, which features fresh seafood, hearty stews, and unique dishes such as curanto, a traditional feast cooked in an underground pit. With its rich cultural heritage and stunning natural landscapes, the Chiloé Archipelago offers a captivating glimpse into the soul of Chile and is not to be missed on any journey through this diverse and enchanting country.

From the soaring peaks of Torres del Paine to the surreal landscapes of the Atacama Desert, Chile's must-see attractions promise unforgettable adventures and unparalleled natural beauty that will leave travelers awe-struck and inspired. Whether exploring ancient ruins on Easter Island, cruising through the icy waters of the

Chilean fjords, or immersing yourself in the vibrant culture of the Chiloé Archipelago, Chile offers a wealth of experiences waiting to be discovered in one of the world's most diverse and captivating destinations.

HUERQUEHUE NATIONAL PARK

EXPLORING SANTIAGO

Santiago, the vibrant capital city of Chile, is a bustling metropolis nestled in a valley surrounded by the snow-capped peaks of the Andes Mountains. With its rich blend of history, culture, and modernity, Santiago offers travelers a captivating mix of old-world charm and cosmopolitan energy waiting to be explored.

1. **Historic Landmarks and Cultural Heritage:** Begin your exploration of Santiago in the city's historic center, where colonial architecture and cobblestone streets harken back to its Spanish colonial past. Plaza de Armas, the city's main square, is a hub of activity and a perfect starting point for your journey. Here, you'll find landmarks such as the majestic Metropolitan Cathedral, the ornate Palacio de la Real Audiencia, and the historic Correo Central building. Take a leisurely stroll through the nearby streets of Barrio Lastarria and Bellavista, where colorful street art, bohemian cafes, and artisan markets await. Don't miss the opportunity to visit La Chascona, the former home of Nobel Prize-winning poet Pablo Neruda, which offers a glimpse into the poet's eclectic lifestyle and love for the arts.

2. **Cultural Institutions and Museums:** Santiago is home to a wealth of cultural institutions and museums that offer insight into Chilean history, art, and heritage. Explore the Museo Chileno de Arte Precolombino, where exhibits showcase the artistic achievements of indigenous cultures from across the Americas, or visit the Museo Nacional de Bellas Artes, which houses an impressive collection of Chilean and international artwork spanning from the colonial period to the present day. For history

enthusiasts, a visit to the Museo Histórico Nacional is a must, offering exhibits on Chile's colonial past, independence movement, and modern history. Additionally, immerse yourself in the local culture by attending a performance at the iconic Teatro Municipal or catching a traditional cueca dance performance at one of Santiago's many cultural venues.

3. **Culinary Delights and Gastronomic Experiences:** No visit to Santiago is complete without sampling the city's diverse culinary offerings and indulging in its gastronomic delights. From hearty traditional dishes like empanadas and cazuela to innovative contemporary cuisine, Santiago's food scene is a reflection of its multicultural heritage and diverse influences. Explore the bustling Mercado Central, where vendors offer fresh seafood and local specialties, or head to the trendy neighborhoods of Barrio Italia and Barrio Yungay, where artisanal cafes and gourmet restaurants abound. Don't forget to pair your meal with a glass of Chilean wine, as Santiago is surrounded by some of the country's most renowned wine-producing regions, including the Maipo and Casablanca Valleys.

4. **Outdoor Escapes and Natural Beauty:** Escape the hustle and bustle of the city and immerse yourself in nature at Santiago's numerous parks and green

spaces. Take a leisurely stroll through Parque Forestal, a picturesque urban park that stretches along the Mapocho River, or hike to the top of Cerro San Cristóbal for panoramic views of the city and the Andes beyond. For a more adventurous experience, venture to the nearby Cajón del Maipo, a stunning river canyon located just outside the city, where you can hike, horseback ride, or simply soak in the natural hot springs. Whatever your interests may be, Santiago offers a wealth of opportunities for exploration and discovery, making it a captivating destination that will leave you enchanted by its charm and beauty.

SANTIAGO DE CHILE

MARVELS OF PATAGONIA

Patagonia, a vast and untamed region spanning the southernmost reaches of Chile and Argentina, is a land of unparalleled natural beauty and dramatic landscapes that captivate the imagination and stir the soul. From towering peaks and sprawling glaciers to pristine fjords and windswept plains, Patagonia offers travelers a wilderness adventure unlike any other, where the spirit of exploration and discovery thrives amidst breathtaking scenery and boundless horizons.

1. **Torres del Paine National Park:** At the heart of Chilean Patagonia lies Torres del Paine National Park, one of the crown jewels of South America's protected areas. Towering granite spires, glacial lakes, and windswept pampas define this iconic landscape, where jagged peaks such as the Torres del Paine and Cuernos del Paine rise dramatically from the earth. Visitors can explore a network of well-marked trails that lead through ancient forests, past cascading waterfalls, and alongside turquoise lakes, offering opportunities to encounter iconic Patagonian wildlife such as guanacos, foxes, and Andean condors. Whether trekking the renowned W Circuit, horseback riding through the rugged terrain, or kayaking amidst floating icebergs, Torres del Paine

promises unforgettable adventures in one of the world's most stunning natural landscapes.

2. **Los Glaciares National Park:** Across the border in Argentine Patagonia lies Los Glaciares National Park, a site renowned for its expansive ice fields, towering glaciers, and rugged mountain scenery. The park's centerpiece is the awe-inspiring Perito Moreno Glacier, a massive ice formation that stretches for miles across the landscape and periodically calves massive icebergs into the turquoise waters of Lake Argentino below. Visitors can experience the glacier up close on boat tours or walking excursions, marveling at its sheer size and dynamic beauty. Additionally, Los Glaciares offers opportunities for hiking, mountaineering, and wildlife viewing, with trails leading through ancient beech forests, past thundering waterfalls, and alongside shimmering lakes where flamingos and other bird species gather in abundance.

3. **Tierra del Fuego National Park:** At the southernmost tip of South America lies Tierra del Fuego National Park, a remote and pristine wilderness area where the rugged landscapes of Patagonia meet the windswept shores of the Beagle Channel. Here, visitors can explore a variety of ecosystems, from lush forests and sub-Antarctic bogs to windswept coastal plains and rugged mountain

peaks. Hiking trails lead through the park's diverse terrain, offering opportunities to encounter native wildlife such as foxes, beavers, and Andean condors, as well as to explore historic sites such as ancient Yámana settlements and the End of the World Train. For those seeking adventure, Tierra del Fuego also offers opportunities for kayaking, canoeing, and fishing in its pristine waterways, as well as for cruising through the Beagle Channel to visit remote islands and wildlife reserves.

4. **The Chilean Fjords and Cape Horn:** For intrepid explorers, a voyage through the Chilean fjords and around Cape Horn offers a once-in-a-lifetime opportunity to experience the remote and rugged landscapes of Patagonia from the deck of a ship. Cruising through narrow channels and sheltered bays, travelers can marvel at towering peaks, emerald forests, and sparkling waterways that define this pristine wilderness. Highlights of the journey include navigating the legendary Strait of Magellan, visiting historic ports such as Punta Arenas and Puerto Williams, and witnessing the dramatic landscapes of Cape Horn, the southernmost point of South America. Along the way, keep an eye out for abundant wildlife, including seals, dolphins, and whales, as well as seabirds such as albatrosses,

petrels, and penguins that call these remote and pristine waters home.

5. **The Paine Massif and Fitz Roy:** For mountaineers and outdoor enthusiasts, the Paine Massif in Chilean Patagonia and Mount Fitz Roy in Argentine Patagonia offer some of the most iconic and challenging climbing routes in the world. Towering granite spires, sheer rock faces, and unpredictable weather conditions define these legendary peaks, where climbers from around the globe come to test their skills and push their limits. The Paine Massif, home to peaks such as Cerro Torre and Cerro Fitz Roy, offers a variety of climbing routes and trekking trails that lead through some of the most stunning and remote landscapes in Patagonia. Similarly, Mount Fitz Roy, known as the "smoking mountain" due to its perpetually cloud-shrouded summit, presents a formidable challenge for climbers and offers unparalleled opportunities for adventure amidst some of the most breathtaking scenery on Earth.

In essence, Patagonia is a land of extremes, where towering peaks, sprawling glaciers, and pristine wilderness define the landscape and inspire a sense of awe and wonder in all who visit. Whether exploring the rugged terrain of Torres del Paine, cruising through the Chilean fjords, or climbing the iconic peaks of Fitz Roy and the Paine Massif, Patagonia offers a wilderness adventure unlike any other, where the spirit of exploration and discovery thrives amidst some of the most stunning natural landscapes on Earth.

PATAGONIA

MYSTERIES OF EASTER ISLAND

Easter Island, or Rapa Nui as it is known to its indigenous inhabitants, is one of the most remote inhabited islands on Earth, located in the southeastern Pacific Ocean. Renowned for its enigmatic moai statues, towering stone monoliths carved by the island's ancient Polynesian inhabitants, Easter Island offers a fascinating glimpse into a mysterious and captivating past that continues to intrigue and mystify travelers from around the world.

1. **The Moai Statues:** The moai statues are perhaps the most iconic and enigmatic feature of Easter Island, standing sentinel against the passage of time and serving as silent guardians of the island's ancient heritage. Carved from solid volcanic rock, these towering monoliths range in size from a few feet to over 30 feet tall and are characterized by their distinctive facial features, elongated noses, and solemn expressions. While the exact purpose of the moai remains a subject of debate among scholars, it is believed that they were erected by the island's early inhabitants to honor their ancestors or tribal chiefs, serving as repositories of ancestral mana, or spiritual power. Today, hundreds of moai statues dot the landscape of Easter Island, standing in silent testament to the ingenuity and creativity of its ancient inhabitants.

2. **Ahu Platforms and Stone Quarries:** Scattered across Easter Island are numerous ahu platforms, stone platforms upon which the moai statues were erected, often in rows facing inland towards the island's interior. These platforms served as ceremonial centers and gathering places for the island's inhabitants, where rituals, ceremonies, and celebrations were held to honor the ancestors and

ensure the prosperity of the community. Surrounding the ahu platforms are the remains of stone quarries where the moai statues were carved, providing insights into the craftsmanship and engineering skills of the island's ancient inhabitants. Here, unfinished statues lie abandoned in various stages of completion, offering a glimpse into the labor-intensive process of quarrying, shaping, and transporting these massive stone monoliths across the island's rugged terrain.

3. **Rano Raraku and the Quarry of the Moai:** At the heart of Easter Island lies Rano Raraku, a volcanic crater that served as the primary quarry for the island's moai statues. Here, hundreds of moai statues lie partially buried in the soft volcanic tuff, with only their heads and torsos exposed to the elements. It is believed that Rano Raraku was not only a quarry but also a sacred site where the moai were imbued with spiritual significance before being transported to their final resting places on the island's coastline. Visitors to Rano Raraku can explore the quarry on foot, marveling at the sheer scale and craftsmanship of the moai statues and pondering the mysteries of their creation and purpose. Additionally, the crater itself offers opportunities for hiking and exploration, with panoramic views of the surrounding landscape and the azure waters of the Pacific Ocean beyond.

4. **Orongo and the Birdman Cult:** Perched atop the cliffs of Easter Island's southwestern coast lies Orongo, a ceremonial village that served as the center of the island's Birdman cult. The cult, which emerged in the wake of the collapse of the island's moai-building civilization, centered around a ritualistic competition known as the "birdman" or "tangata manu" ceremony. Each year, representatives from the island's competing clans would gather at Orongo to compete in a perilous race to retrieve the first egg laid by the migratory sooty tern from the nearby islet of Motu Nui. The winner of the competition would be declared the "birdman" for the following year, bestowing prestige and power upon their clan. Today, visitors to Orongo can explore the remains of the ceremonial village, including the stone houses, petroglyphs, and ceremonial platforms that bear witness to this ancient and fascinating tradition.

5. **The Decline of Easter Island's Civilization:** The decline of Easter Island's ancient civilization remains one of the most enduring mysteries of the island's history. Scholars believe that environmental degradation, resource depletion, and societal upheaval played a significant role in the collapse of the island's moai-building culture, leading to social unrest, famine, and population decline. Deforestation, caused by the island's early inhabitants for the

purpose of clearing land for agriculture and transporting the massive moai statues, resulted in soil erosion, loss of biodiversity, and a decline in agricultural productivity. This, combined with the introduction of Invasive species such as rats, further exacerbated the island's ecological crisis, leading to the collapse of its once-thriving civilization. Today, the legacy of Easter Island's ancient inhabitants serves as a cautionary tale about the importance of environmental stewardship and sustainable resource management in an increasingly interconnected world.

In a nutshell, Easter Island is a place of profound mystery and intrigue, where the enigmatic moai statues stand as silent sentinels of a bygone era and the remnants of an ancient civilization bear witness to the complexities of human history. Whether exploring the quarry of Rano Raraku, marveling at the birdman petroglyphs of Orongo, or pondering the mysteries of the island's decline, Easter Island offers a journey into the heart of an ancient and captivating past that continues to inspire wonder and fascination to this day.

CHAPTER FOUR
WHERE TO STAY

Choosing the right accommodation is essential for a memorable and comfortable stay in Chile. From luxury resorts and boutique hotels to budget-friendly hostels and eco-lodges, Chile offers a diverse range of lodging options to suit every traveler's preferences and budget. In Santiago, the capital city, visitors can find a wide array of accommodations ranging from upscale hotels in the bustling city center to charming bed and breakfasts in the historic neighborhoods of Lastarria and Bellavista. For those seeking a beach getaway, the coastal towns of Viña del Mar and Valparaíso offer a variety of seaside resorts and boutique hotels with stunning ocean views and easy access to the region's sandy beaches and vibrant nightlife.

In Chilean Patagonia, travelers can choose from a range of accommodation options that allow them to immerse themselves in the region's pristine wilderness and breathtaking landscapes. From luxury lodges and all-inclusive resorts to rustic cabins and wilderness campsites, there are lodging options to suit every style of traveler and budget. Whether staying in the heart of Torres del Paine National Park or exploring the remote fjords and glaciers of the Chilean coast, Patagonia offers unforgettable accommodation experiences that complement the region's natural beauty and outdoor adventures.

RÍO BLANCO

BOUTIQUE HOTELS AND RESORTS IN CHILE

Chile, with its diverse landscapes and rich cultural heritage, offers travelers a wealth of boutique hotels and resorts that combine luxury amenities with authentic local charm. From the bustling streets of Santiago to the pristine wilderness of Patagonia, these boutique accommodations provide a unique and immersive experience that allows guests to connect with the natural beauty and cultural richness of the region.

1. **The Singular Santiago:** Located in the heart of Santiago's historic Lastarria neighborhood, The Singular Santiago is a boutique hotel housed in a beautifully restored 20th-century building. With its elegant architecture, contemporary design, and curated collection of artwork and artifacts, the hotel offers a sophisticated retreat in the heart of the city. Guests can relax in stylishly appointed rooms and suites, dine on innovative Chilean cuisine at the hotel's restaurant, and unwind with a cocktail at the rooftop bar, which offers panoramic views of the city skyline and the nearby Andes Mountains. The Singular Santiago also offers a range of amenities, including a fitness center, spa, and outdoor swimming pool, making it the perfect base for exploring Santiago's cultural attractions, culinary delights, and vibrant nightlife.

2. **Awasi Patagonia:** Nestled in the pristine wilderness of Torres del Paine National Park, Awasi Patagonia is a luxury resort that offers guests a secluded and immersive experience in one of the world's most stunning natural landscapes. The resort features a collection of private villas, each with its own wood-burning stove, outdoor hot tub, and panoramic views of the surrounding mountains and glaciers. Guests can enjoy personalized excursions led by expert guides, including hiking, horseback riding, and wildlife watching, as well as gourmet meals prepared with locally sourced ingredients and paired with fine Chilean wines. With its commitment to sustainability and conservation, Awasi Patagonia provides a responsible and eco-friendly approach to luxury travel, allowing guests to connect with nature while minimizing their impact on the environment.

3. **Tierra Atacama Hotel & Spa:** Set against the backdrop of the otherworldly Atacama Desert, Tierra Atacama Hotel & Spa is a boutique retreat that offers guests an oasis of luxury and tranquility in one of Chile's most remote and captivating landscapes. The hotel features a collection of stylishly designed rooms and suites, each with its own private terrace overlooking the desert landscape. Guests can indulge in holistic spa treatments inspired by ancient indigenous healing traditions, dine on gourmet

cuisine prepared with locally sourced ingredients, and relax by the outdoor swimming pool or in the rooftop hot tubs, which offer panoramic views of the surrounding volcanoes and salt flats. Tierra Atacama also offers a range of guided excursions, including stargazing, desert hikes, and visits to local villages and archaeological sites, allowing guests to immerse themselves in the culture and natural beauty of the Atacama Desert.

4. **Casa Higueras:** Perched atop the hills of Valparaíso, Casa Higueras is a boutique hotel that offers guests a unique blend of historic charm and modern luxury in one of Chile's most vibrant and colorful cities. Housed in a beautifully restored 1920s mansion, the hotel features elegantly appointed rooms and suites, each with its own unique décor and breathtaking views of the city and the nearby Pacific Ocean. Guests can dine on gourmet cuisine at the hotel's restaurant, relax by the outdoor swimming pool surrounded by lush gardens, or explore the city's historic landmarks and artistic treasures with the help of the hotel's knowledgeable concierge. With its intimate atmosphere, personalized service, and commitment to sustainability, Casa Higueras provides a tranquil and welcoming retreat in the heart of Valparaíso's historic quarter.

5. **Vik Chile:** Situated in the Millahue Valley of Chile's Colchagua wine region, Vik Chile is a luxurious boutique retreat that combines contemporary design, world-class art, and breathtaking views of the surrounding vineyards and Andes Mountains. The hotel features a collection of avant-garde suites and villas, each uniquely designed by renowned architects and artists, with amenities such as private plunge pools, outdoor showers, and expansive terraces. Guests can enjoy personalized wine tastings and vineyard tours, dine on farm-to-table cuisine at the hotel's gourmet restaurant, and unwind with holistic spa treatments inspired by the healing powers of the land. With its commitment to sustainability and environmental stewardship, Vik Chile offers guests a responsible and eco-conscious approach to luxury travel, allowing them to immerse themselves in the beauty and tranquility of Chile's wine country while minimizing their impact on the environment.

6. **Hacienda Vira Vira:** Nestled amidst the lush forests and snow-capped volcanoes of Chile's Lake District, Hacienda Vira Vira is an exclusive boutique hotel and working farm that offers guests a unique opportunity to experience rural life in one of Chile's most picturesque regions. The hotel features a collection of cozy suites and villas, each with its own fireplace, outdoor terrace, and panoramic views of

the surrounding countryside. Guests can participate in a variety of activities, including horseback riding, fly fishing, and farm-to-table cooking classes, as well as enjoy gourmet cuisine prepared with organic ingredients sourced from the hotel's own gardens and dairy farm. With its commitment to sustainable agriculture and community development, Hacienda Vira Vira provides guests with an authentic and immersive experience that celebrates the natural beauty and cultural heritage of the Lake District.

7. **Explora Patagonia:** Located on the shores of Lake Pehoé in Torres del Paine National Park, Explora Patagonia is a luxury adventure lodge that offers guests unparalleled access to one of the world's most remote and pristine wilderness areas. The lodge features a collection of modernist-style rooms and suites, each with floor-to-ceiling windows and breathtaking views of the surrounding mountains and glaciers. Guests can choose from a variety of guided excursions, including hiking, horseback riding, and boat tours, led by expert guides who share their knowledge and passion for the region's natural and cultural heritage. After a day of adventure, guests can relax in the lodge's outdoor hot tubs, enjoy gourmet cuisine prepared with locally sourced ingredients, and unwind with a massage or yoga session in the on-site spa. With its commitment to sustainable

tourism and conservation, Explora Patagonia offers guests a responsible and eco-friendly way to experience the wonders of Chile's southern wilderness.

In essence, Chile's boutique hotels and resorts offer travelers a luxurious and authentic way to experience the country's diverse landscapes and rich cultural heritage. Whether exploring the vineyards of Colchagua, the forests of the Lake District, or the wilderness of Patagonia, these boutique accommodations provide an unforgettable blend of comfort, style, and local hospitality that will leave guests feeling pampered, rejuvenated, and inspired.

VALPARAÍSO

BUDGET-FRIENDLY ACCOMMODATIONS

Traveling on a budget doesn't mean sacrificing comfort or convenience, especially in a country as diverse and welcoming as Chile. From vibrant cities to remote wilderness areas, Chile offers a range of budget-friendly accommodations that cater to the needs of thrifty travelers without compromising on quality or experience. Whether you're backpacking through Patagonia, exploring the streets of Santiago, or soaking up the sun on the beaches of the Pacific coast, there are plenty of options for affordable lodging that allow you to make the most of your travel budget while still enjoying all that Chile has to offer.

HOSTELS AND GUESTHOUSES

- **Rado Boutique Hostel (Santiago):** Located in the vibrant Bellavista neighborhood, this stylish hostel offers dormitory beds and private rooms at affordable rates. Amenities include free Wi-Fi, a communal kitchen, and a rooftop terrace with views of the city.
- **La Bohème Hostel (Valparaíso):** Situated in the heart of Valparaíso's UNESCO-listed historic quarter, this cozy hostel features colorful dormitories and private rooms with shared bathrooms. Guests can enjoy a complimentary breakfast, free Wi-Fi, and a communal lounge with a fireplace.

- **Erratic Rock II (Puerto Natales):** A popular choice for travelers heading to Torres del Paine National Park, this friendly hostel offers comfortable dormitory beds and private rooms with shared facilities. The hostel also organizes guided tours and trekking expeditions to the park.
- **Atacama Hostel (San Pedro de Atacama):** Nestled in the heart of San Pedro de Atacama, this charming hostel offers budget-friendly accommodations in a relaxed and social atmosphere. Guests can enjoy a communal kitchen, outdoor patio, and organized excursions to nearby attractions such as the Atacama Salt Flat and Valle de la Luna.

CAMPING AND REFUGIOS

- **Torres del Paine National Park (Patagonia):** The park offers a range of designated campsites and mountain refuges where travelers can pitch a tent or stay in basic mountain huts. Amenities vary by location but may include cooking facilities, restrooms, and potable water.
- **Lauca National Park (Andean Altiplano):** Located in northern Chile, Lauca National Park offers several campsites and refugios for budget-conscious travelers exploring the high-altitude landscapes of the Andes. Facilities are basic but

provide stunning views of the park's snow-capped volcanoes and highland lagoons.

- **Chiloé National Park (Chiloé Archipelago):** Travelers visiting Chiloé National Park can camp at designated campsites or stay in rustic refugios nestled amidst the park's temperate rainforests and coastal wetlands. Facilities may be limited, so visitors should come prepared with camping gear and supplies.

BUDGET HOTELS AND GUESTHOUSES

- **Hotel Foresta (Santiago):** Situated in the bustling Providencia neighborhood, this budget-friendly hotel offers comfortable rooms with private bathrooms, flat-screen TVs, and free Wi-Fi. Guests can enjoy a complimentary breakfast buffet and convenient access to public transportation.
- **Hostal Entre Vientos (Puerto Varas):** Located near the shores of Lake Llanquihue, this cozy guesthouse offers affordable accommodations in a tranquil setting. Rooms feature wooden furnishings, private bathrooms, and views of the surrounding gardens or lake.
- **Hostal Nalhuitad (Puerto Montt):** A short walk from the city center, this budget-friendly guesthouse offers simple yet comfortable rooms with private bathrooms and complimentary Wi-Fi. Guests can

relax in the communal lounge or explore nearby attractions such as Angelmó Market and Tenglo Island.

AIRBNB AND VACATION RENTALS

- **Cozy Apartment in Providencia (Santiago):** This affordable Airbnb rental offers a cozy studio apartment with a fully equipped kitchen, private bathroom, and complimentary Wi-Fi. Located in the trendy Providencia neighborhood, guests can enjoy easy access to restaurants, cafes, and public transportation.

- **Ocean View Studio in Viña del Mar:** Perfect for budget-conscious travelers, this Airbnb rental offers a studio apartment with stunning ocean views, a private balcony, and access to a rooftop swimming pool. Guests can explore the nearby beaches and attractions of Viña del Mar at their leisure.

- **Cabin in the Woods near Pucón:** Ideal for outdoor enthusiasts, this secluded cabin rental offers rustic accommodations amidst the forests and mountains near Pucón. Guests can enjoy hiking, fishing, and birdwatching in the surrounding wilderness, with the town of Pucón just a short drive away for dining and shopping options.

These budget-friendly accommodations provide travelers with affordable options for exploring Chile's diverse landscapes, vibrant cities, and cultural attractions without breaking the bank. Whether you're backpacking through Patagonia, exploring the streets of Santiago, or relaxing on the beaches of the Pacific coast, there's a budget-friendly lodging option to suit every traveler's needs and preferences.

ATACAMA

UNIQUE STAYS

Chile, with its diverse landscapes and rich cultural heritage, offers travelers a wide range of unique and memorable accommodation options that go beyond the traditional hotel experience. From remote eco-lodges and historic haciendas to luxury tents and treehouses, these one-of-a-kind stays provide guests with the opportunity to immerse themselves in the natural beauty and cultural richness of Chile while enjoying unparalleled comfort and hospitality.

1. **Eco-Lodges in Patagonia:** Nestled amidst the pristine wilderness of Chilean Patagonia, eco-lodges offer travelers a sustainable and immersive way to experience the region's stunning landscapes and diverse ecosystems. Properties such as Patagonia Camp in Torres del Paine National Park and EcoCamp Patagonia in the heart of the park offer luxurious tented accommodations with panoramic views of the surrounding mountains and glaciers. Guests can enjoy guided excursions to explore the park's hiking trails, kayaking routes, and wildlife viewing spots, as well as indulge in gourmet cuisine prepared with locally sourced ingredients and relax in eco-friendly amenities such as outdoor hot tubs and yoga platforms.

2. **Historic Haciendas in the Atacama Desert:** In the vast and otherworldly landscapes of the Atacama Desert, historic haciendas offer travelers a glimpse into Chile's colonial past and the traditional way of life in the region. Properties such as Hacienda Juntas in the oasis town of San Pedro de Atacama and Hacienda Los Andes in the desert foothills offer charming accommodations in beautifully restored colonial-era buildings surrounded by lush gardens and vineyards. Guests can explore the surrounding desert landscapes on horseback or mountain bike, visit nearby archaeological sites and indigenous villages, and relax with traditional Andean cuisine and regional wines served in elegant dining rooms or al fresco patios.

3. **Luxury Glamping in the Lake District:** For travelers seeking a unique and indulgent experience in Chile's Lake District, luxury glamping offers the perfect combination of comfort and adventure amidst the region's breathtaking natural beauty. Properties such as Patagonia Camp on the shores of Lake Toro and Nomades Hotel Boutique in the Chiloé Archipelago offer spacious and stylishly appointed tents with plush bedding, en-suite bathrooms, and private terraces with panoramic views of the surrounding landscapes. Guests can enjoy a range of outdoor activities, including kayaking, fly fishing,

and birdwatching, as well as relax with gourmet meals prepared with locally sourced ingredients and unwind with spa treatments and yoga sessions in serene natural settings.

4. **Treehouses in the Valdivian Rainforest:** For a truly unforgettable stay in Chile's pristine wilderness, treehouses offer a unique and immersive way to connect with nature and experience the magic of the forest canopy. Properties such as Huilo Huilo Biological Reserve in the Valdivian Rainforest and La Montaña Mágica Lodge in the Andean foothills offer rustic yet luxurious accommodations in treehouses perched high above the forest floor. Guests can enjoy panoramic views of the surrounding landscapes, observe native wildlife such as monkeys and toucans from their treetop hideaways, and explore the forest on guided hikes, canopy tours, and wildlife spotting excursions. With their secluded locations, eco-friendly amenities, and intimate atmosphere, treehouses provide guests with a truly magical and unforgettable stay in the heart of Chile's natural wonders.

5. **Island Retreats in Chiloé Archipelago:** In the remote and enchanting landscapes of the Chiloé Archipelago, island retreats offer travelers a peaceful and secluded escape from the hustle and bustle of modern life. Properties such as Tierra Chiloé Hotel &

Spa on the island of Chiloé and Refugia Lodge on the island of Rauco offer elegant accommodations in harmony with their natural surroundings, with panoramic views of the Pacific Ocean and nearby islands. Guests can explore the archipelago's unique cultural heritage, including its iconic wooden churches and traditional palafitos (stilt houses), as well as enjoy outdoor activities such as kayaking, birdwatching, and horseback riding. With their warm hospitality, locally inspired cuisine, and commitment to sustainability, island retreats provide guests with a tranquil and rejuvenating experience in one of Chile's most captivating destinations.

In essence, unique stays in Chile offer travelers the opportunity to experience the country's diverse landscapes and cultural heritage in unforgettable ways. Whether staying in an eco-lodge in Patagonia, a historic hacienda in the Atacama Desert, a luxury tent in the Lake District, a treehouse in the Valdivian Rainforest, or an island retreat in the Chiloé Archipelago, these one-of-a-kind accommodations provide guests with an immersive and enriching experience that celebrates the natural beauty and cultural richness of Chile.

CHAPTER FIVE
OUTDOOR ACTIVITIES

Chile's diverse landscapes offer endless opportunities for outdoor adventure enthusiasts. From the rugged peaks of the Andes to the pristine wilderness of Patagonia and the remote islands of the Pacific coast, Chile is a playground for those who love to explore the great outdoors. Whether you're seeking adrenaline-pumping activities like trekking and whitewater rafting or more leisurely pursuits such as birdwatching and stargazing, there's something for everyone to enjoy amidst Chile's natural wonders.

Embark on a multi-day trek through the iconic Torres del Paine National Park, where you'll encounter towering granite spires, turquoise lakes, and sweeping valleys carved by ancient glaciers. For thrill-seekers, whitewater rafting on the wild and scenic Futaleufú River offers an exhilarating ride through Class III and IV rapids against the backdrop of the Andean mountains. Alternatively, explore the mystical landscapes of the Atacama Desert on a guided hiking or biking tour, where you'll discover otherworldly salt flats, geothermal hot springs, and lunar-like landscapes reminiscent of Mars. Whether you're an experienced adventurer or a novice explorer, Chile's outdoor activities promise an unforgettable journey into the heart of nature's beauty and grandeur.

TORRES DEL PAINE NATIONAL PARK

HIKING IN THE ATACAMA DESERT

The Atacama Desert, often referred to as the driest desert in the world, is a surreal landscape of otherworldly beauty and stark contrasts. While it may seem barren and inhospitable at first glance, the desert is teeming with life and geological wonders waiting to be explored. One of the most popular activities for visitors to the Atacama Desert is hiking, offering an intimate and immersive way to experience the unique landscapes and natural phenomena of this extraordinary region.

- **Moon Valley (Valle de la Luna):** One of the most iconic and mesmerizing destinations in the Atacama Desert is Moon Valley, or Valle de la Luna. Named for its lunar-like landscapes and eerie rock formations, this otherworldly valley is a testament to the power of wind and water erosion over millions of years. Hiking through Moon Valley feels like stepping onto another planet, with towering sand dunes, jagged rock formations, and salt-crusted valleys stretching as far as the eye can see. Visitors can explore the valley on a network of well-marked trails, ranging from easy strolls to more challenging hikes that lead to panoramic viewpoints overlooking the vast expanse of the desert below. Highlights of a hike through Moon Valley include the iconic "Duna

Mayor" sand dune, the surreal "Amphitheater" rock formation, and the otherworldly "Salt Caves," where salt crystals sparkle like diamonds in the desert sunlight.

- **Salt Flats (Salar de Atacama):** Another must-see destination for hikers in the Atacama Desert is the Salar de Atacama, or Atacama Salt Flat, the largest salt flat in Chile and one of the largest in the world. Stretching for over 3,000 square kilometers, this vast expanse of salt crust is a mesmerizing sight to behold, shimmering with shades of white and pink beneath the intense desert sun. Hiking across the salt flats is like walking on another planet, with the crunch of salt crystals beneath your feet and the endless expanse of the desert stretching to the horizon in every direction. Along the way, hikers may encounter otherworldly rock formations, volcanic craters, and natural salt lagoons teeming with flamingos and other birdlife. One of the highlights of hiking in the salt flats is witnessing the breathtaking beauty of the sunset, as the colors of the desert sky are reflected in the mirror-like surface of the salt crust, creating a truly magical and unforgettable experience.

In shorts, hiking in the Atacama Desert offers adventurers a unique opportunity to explore some of the most surreal and captivating landscapes on Earth. From the lunar-like landscapes of Moon Valley to the shimmering salt flats of Salar de Atacama, hikers can immerse themselves in the natural beauty and geological wonders of this extraordinary region, forging a deeper connection with the land and its ancient mysteries along the way. Whether you're an experienced trekker or a novice explorer, hiking in the Atacama Desert promises an unforgettable journey into the heart of one of the world's most enchanting and enigmatic landscapes.

ADVENTURE SPORTS IN PUCON

Pucón, nestled in the heart of Chile's Lake District, is renowned as an adventure sports paradise, attracting thrill-seekers and outdoor enthusiasts from around the world. With its stunning natural landscapes, including pristine lakes, lush forests, and towering volcanoes, Pucón offers a wide range of adrenaline-pumping activities that cater to all levels of experience and skill. From navigating whitewater rapids to trekking through ancient forests and summiting active volcanoes, Pucón promises an unforgettable adventure for those seeking excitement and exploration.

- **Whitewater Rafting:** One of the most popular adventure sports in Pucón is whitewater rafting, offering an exhilarating ride down the region's wild and scenic rivers. The nearby Trancura River, with its Class III and IV rapids, provides the perfect playground for adrenaline junkies and novice rafters alike. Experienced guides lead thrilling rafting excursions that navigate through churning rapids, steep drops, and rocky obstacles, ensuring a safe and unforgettable adventure for all participants. Along the way, rafters can enjoy breathtaking views of the surrounding forests, mountains, and volcanic landscapes, with opportunities to spot native wildlife such as birds, fish, and even the occasional Andean condor soaring overhead.

- **Trekking:** For those seeking a more immersive and exploratory adventure, trekking through the forests and mountains surrounding Pucón offers a chance to connect with nature and discover hidden gems off the beaten path. The nearby Villarrica National Park, home to the iconic Villarrica Volcano, boasts a network of well-marked hiking trails that lead through ancient Araucaria forests, past sparkling mountain lakes, and up to breathtaking viewpoints overlooking the surrounding landscapes. Experienced guides lead guided trekking excursions that cater to all levels of fitness and experience, from leisurely strolls to challenging multi-day hikes. Highlights of trekking in the area include the picturesque Ojos del Caburgua waterfalls, the tranquil shores of Lake

Huerquehue, and the awe-inspiring summit of Villarrica Volcano, where adventurous hikers can peer into the steaming crater and take in panoramic views of the surrounding Andes.

- **Volcano Climbing:** For the ultimate adventure experience in Pucón, nothing beats the thrill of summiting an active volcano. Villarrica Volcano, one of Chile's most iconic and active volcanoes, offers experienced climbers a challenging and unforgettable ascent to its snow-capped summit. Guided volcano climbing expeditions lead participants through rugged terrain, past smoking fumaroles, and up steep snow and ice slopes to reach the crater rim, where they can peer into the fiery depths of the volcano and take in sweeping views of the surrounding landscapes. Climbing Villarrica Volcano requires a good level of physical fitness and mountaineering experience, as well as proper equipment such as crampons, ice axes, and helmets. However, for those who are up to the challenge, the sense of accomplishment and the breathtaking views from the summit make it a once-in-a-lifetime adventure that will be remembered for years to come.

In essence, Pucón offers a diverse range of adventure sports and outdoor activities that cater to all tastes and preferences, from thrilling whitewater rafting trips to scenic treks through ancient forests and challenging climbs up active volcanoes. Whether you're an adrenaline junkie seeking excitement or a nature lover looking to connect with the great outdoors, Pucón promises an unforgettable adventure experience that will leave you exhilarated, inspired, and longing to return for more.

ATACAMA

WILDLIFE ENCOUNTERS

Chile is home to an astonishing array of wildlife, from majestic marine mammals to colorful bird species that inhabit its diverse ecosystems. Two of the most remarkable wildlife encounters that visitors can experience in Chile are whale watching in Chiloé and birdwatching in Lauca National Park. These experiences offer nature lovers and wildlife enthusiasts the chance to witness some of the country's most iconic and captivating creatures in their natural habitats, providing unforgettable opportunities for observation, appreciation, and conservation.

- **Whale Watching in Chiloé:** Off the coast of Chiloé, a picturesque archipelago in southern Chile, lies one of the best whale watching destinations in the world. Each year, from December to March, southern right whales migrate to the nutrient-rich waters of the Pacific Ocean to breed and give birth, providing visitors with a unique opportunity to observe these magnificent creatures up close. Guided whale watching tours depart from the island's coastal towns, taking visitors out into the open sea aboard small boats equipped with experienced guides and spotters who know where to find the whales. As the boats venture into deeper waters, passengers may encounter not only southern right whales but also other species such as humpback whales, blue whales, and orcas, as well as playful dolphins and seals. Watching these majestic marine mammals breach, spy-hop, and slap their tails against the water's surface is an awe-inspiring experience that leaves a lasting impression on all who witness it, while also raising awareness about the importance of protecting these vulnerable creatures and their marine habitats.

- **Birdwatching in Lauca National Park:** Nestled high in the Andean highlands of northern Chile, Lauca National Park is a paradise for birdwatchers, with its diverse habitats ranging from high-altitude grasslands and wetlands to rugged mountain slopes and volcanic peaks. The park is home to an impressive variety of bird species, including endemic and endangered species that are found nowhere else on Earth. Guided birdwatching tours lead visitors through the park's pristine landscapes, where they can spot a wide range of avian species such as the Andean condor, Chilean flamingo, puna ibis, and Andean gull, as well as colorful hummingbirds, finches, and tanagers. One of the highlights of birdwatching in Lauca National Park is visiting the Chungará Lake, a stunning high-altitude lake that serves as a crucial habitat for numerous bird species, including waterfowl, shorebirds, and migratory species that visit the park during the austral summer.

Watching flocks of flamingos wading through the shallows, Andean geese soaring overhead, and elusive condors circling the peaks of the surrounding volcanoes is a magical experience that immerses visitors in the natural beauty and biodiversity of the Andean highlands, while also promoting conservation efforts to protect these fragile ecosystems and the species that depend on them.

In essence, wildlife encounters in Chile offer visitors the chance to connect with nature and witness some of the country's most remarkable and iconic creatures in their natural habitats. Whether watching whales off the coast of Chiloé or spotting birds in Lauca National Park, these experiences provide unforgettable opportunities for observation, appreciation, and conservation, while also raising awareness about the importance of protecting Chile's diverse ecosystems and the wildlife that call them home.

CHAPTER SIX
CULINARY DELIGHTS

Chilean cuisine is a delightful fusion of indigenous traditions, European influences, and local ingredients sourced from the country's diverse landscapes, ranging from the fertile valleys of central Chile to the bountiful seas of the Pacific coast. Chapter Six explores the culinary delights of Chile, inviting readers on a gastronomic journey through the country's vibrant markets, bustling street food stalls, and acclaimed restaurants. From savory empanadas and hearty cazuelas to fresh ceviche and succulent seafood, Chilean cuisine offers a tantalizing array of flavors and dishes that reflect the country's rich cultural heritage and culinary diversity.

Indulge your senses and tantalize your taste buds with Chile's culinary delights, where every dish tells a story and every bite is a celebration of tradition, innovation, and local flavors. Discover the secrets of traditional Chilean recipes handed down through generations, savor the freshness of locally sourced ingredients, and immerse yourself in the rich tapestry of flavors, aromas, and textures that make Chilean cuisine a true culinary treasure. Whether sampling street food in Santiago, dining in a cozy seafood restaurant in Valparaíso, or exploring the flavors of the Mapuche culture in the

Araucanía region, Chapter Six invites readers to experience the best of Chile's culinary heritage and embark on a culinary adventure that will delight the senses and nourish the soul.

PATAGONIA CHILENA

CHILEAN CUISINE 101

Chilean cuisine is a rich tapestry of flavors, influenced by the country's diverse geography, indigenous cultures, and immigrant communities. From the coastal regions to the Andean highlands, Chile's culinary traditions reflect the abundance of fresh ingredients sourced from land and sea, resulting in a unique and delicious gastronomic experience. In this exploration of Chilean cuisine, we delve into the iconic dishes that define the country's culinary identity, from savory empanadas to comforting pastel de choclo.

1. **Empanadas:** Arguably one of Chile's most beloved and iconic dishes, empanadas are savory pastries filled with a variety of delicious fillings. The dough is typically made from flour, water, and lard, resulting in a flaky and golden crust that encases a flavorful filling. Traditional fillings include seasoned ground beef, onions, olives, and hard-boiled eggs, although there are countless regional variations that incorporate ingredients such as seafood, cheese, and vegetables. Empanadas are a popular street food snack enjoyed throughout Chile, often accompanied by ají sauce for added flavor and spice. Whether enjoyed as a quick bite on the go or as part of a leisurely meal, empanadas are a quintessential

Chilean dish that embodies the country's culinary heritage and cultural diversity.

2. **Pastel de Choclo:** Another staple of Chilean cuisine, pastel de choclo is a hearty and comforting dish that is reminiscent of a savory corn pie. The dish features a thick layer of ground corn (choclo) mixed with onions, garlic, and spices, which is spread over a filling of seasoned meat, chicken, or vegetables. The filling is then topped with a layer of sliced hard-boiled eggs, olives, and sometimes raisins, before being baked until golden and bubbly. Pastel de choclo is a popular dish for family gatherings and special occasions, often served with a side of ensalada chilena (Chilean salad) and accompanied by a glass of Chilean wine or a traditional pisco sour. With its comforting flavors and satisfying texture, pastel de choclo is a true Chilean classic that has been passed down through generations, bringing joy and warmth to tables across the country.

3. **Cazuela de Vacuno:** Cazuela de vacuno is a hearty and comforting stew that is a staple of Chilean cuisine, particularly during the cooler months. This traditional dish features tender chunks of beef simmered with potatoes, pumpkin, corn, rice, and vegetables such as carrots, onions, and bell peppers. The stew is seasoned with herbs and spices such as cilantro, oregano, and cumin, giving it a rich and

aromatic flavor. Cazuela de vacuno is often enjoyed as a main course for lunch or dinner, accompanied by a side of bread or rice. Its hearty and nourishing qualities make it a popular choice for family meals and special occasions, bringing people together to share in its delicious warmth and flavor.

4. **Chilean Seafood:** Given Chile's extensive coastline, it's no surprise that seafood plays a prominent role in the country's cuisine. From fresh fish and shellfish to hearty seafood stews and ceviche, Chile offers a bounty of delicious marine delights. Some of the most popular seafood dishes in Chile include paila marina, a rich seafood soup made with a variety of fish, shellfish, and vegetables; machas a la parmesana, razor clams topped with cheese and baked to perfection; and chupe de mariscos, a creamy seafood casserole made with shrimp, mussels, and crab. Chilean seafood is celebrated for its freshness and flavor, with dishes often featuring locally caught ingredients sourced from the country's abundant coastal waters.

5. **Chilean Wine:** No exploration of Chilean cuisine would be complete without mentioning the country's world-renowned wine industry. Chile is one of the largest producers of wine in the world, with a diverse range of grape varieties and wine styles that reflect the country's unique terroir and microclimates. Some

of the most popular wine regions in Chile include the Maipo Valley, Casablanca Valley, and Colchagua Valley, where vineyards produce high-quality wines such as Cabernet Sauvignon, Carmenere, and Sauvignon Blanc. Wine is an integral part of Chilean culture and cuisine, with meals often accompanied by a glass of local wine or a traditional pisco sour cocktail made with Chilean grape brandy. Whether enjoyed as an aperitif or paired with a delicious meal, Chilean wine adds a special touch to any dining experience, inviting diners to savor the flavors and aromas of this beautiful country.

In a nutshell, Chilean cuisine is a delightful fusion of flavors, ingredients, and culinary traditions that reflect the country's rich cultural heritage and diverse landscapes. From savory empanadas and comforting stews to fresh seafood and world-class wine, Chile offers a gastronomic adventure that is sure to delight the senses and nourish the soul. Whether enjoyed at a local restaurant, a street food stall, or a family dinner table, Chilean cuisine invites diners to experience the warmth, hospitality, and flavor of this beautiful country in every bite.

WINE TASTING IN THE COLCHAGUA VALLEY

Nestled in the heart of Chile's wine country, the Colchagua Valley is renowned for its picturesque vineyards, award-winning wineries, and world-class wines. Located just a few hours' drive south of Santiago, this fertile valley boasts a Mediterranean climate, fertile soils, and a unique terroir that is ideal for grape cultivation. Visitors to the Colchagua Valley are treated to an immersive wine tasting experience that showcases the region's rich viticultural heritage, innovative winemaking techniques, and diverse array of varietals.

1. **Vineyard Tours:** One of the highlights of wine tasting in the Colchagua Valley is touring the region's renowned vineyards, where visitors can learn about the winemaking process from grape to glass. Guided tours of the vineyards provide an opportunity to stroll through the lush vineyards, explore the winery facilities, and discover the history and traditions of winemaking in the Colchagua Valley. Knowledgeable guides offer insights into the unique characteristics of the valley's terroir, grape varietals, and winemaking techniques, while also sharing stories about the families and artisans who have shaped the region's wine industry. Visitors can also witness firsthand the care and craftsmanship that goes into producing each bottle of wine, from hand-

harvesting the grapes to barrel aging and bottling the finished product. Some of the most popular vineyards to visit in the Colchagua Valley include Viu Manent, Montes, Lapostolle, and Casa Silva, each offering its own unique blend of history, tradition, and innovation.

2. **Wine Tastings:** No visit to the Colchagua Valley would be complete without indulging in a wine tasting experience, where visitors can sample a variety of wines that showcase the region's unique terroir and grape varietals. Tastings typically include a selection of red, white, and sparkling wines, ranging from crisp Sauvignon Blancs and aromatic Chardonnays to bold Cabernet Sauvignons and smooth Carménères. Knowledgeable sommeliers guide guests through the tasting process, offering insights into the characteristics of each wine, including aroma, flavor profile, and aging potential. Visitors can also learn about food and wine pairings, regional wine trends, and the art of wine appreciation, all while enjoying stunning views of the surrounding vineyards and valley. Whether sampling wines in a rustic cellar, a modern tasting room, or a scenic outdoor terrace, wine tasting in the Colchagua Valley is a sensory journey that delights the palate and deepens appreciation for Chile's rich winemaking heritage.

3. **Culinary Experiences:** In addition to wine tastings, many wineries in the Colchagua Valley offer culinary experiences that pair their wines with delicious local cuisine. Visitors can enjoy gourmet meals prepared with fresh, seasonal ingredients sourced from the valley's bountiful farms and markets, complemented by carefully selected wine pairings that enhance the flavors of each dish. From traditional Chilean dishes such as empanadas and pastel de choclo to international fare with a local twist, the culinary offerings in the Colchagua Valley are sure to tantalize the taste buds and satisfy even the most discerning palate. Some wineries also offer cooking classes, where visitors can learn to prepare traditional Chilean dishes under the guidance of expert chefs, using fresh ingredients and techniques that highlight the flavors of the region. Whether dining al fresco in a vineyard setting, enjoying a casual picnic lunch, or indulging in a multi-course tasting menu, culinary experiences in the Colchagua Valley are a celebration of the region's rich gastronomic heritage and the perfect complement to a day of wine tasting and exploration.

In essence, wine tasting in the Colchagua Valley offers visitors a unique opportunity to explore Chile's vibrant wine culture, discover the beauty of the valley's vineyards, and savor the flavors of its world-class wines. Whether touring vineyards, sampling wines, or indulging in culinary delights, visitors to the Colchagua Valley are treated to an unforgettable experience that celebrates the rich history, tradition, and innovation of Chilean winemaking. So raise a glass, toast to the beauty of the Colchagua Valley, and savor every moment of this truly memorable wine tasting adventure. Cheers!

SALTO DEL LAJA

SEAFOOD EXTRAVAGANZA

Chile's long coastline and abundant marine resources make it a seafood lover's paradise, offering an array of fresh and flavorful dishes that showcase the country's rich maritime heritage. Among the many seafood delights that Chile has to offer, ceviche and Chilean sea bass stand out as two iconic dishes that are beloved by locals and visitors alike. From the vibrant flavors of citrus-marinated raw fish to the delicate texture of pan-seared sea bass, a seafood extravaganza in Chile promises a culinary experience that is both delicious and unforgettable.

- **Ceviche:** Ceviche is a quintessential dish in Chilean cuisine, celebrated for its bright and refreshing flavors that highlight the natural sweetness and freshness of the seafood. The dish typically consists of raw fish, such as sea bass or salmon, that is marinated in a citrus-based mixture of lemon or lime juice, along with onions, cilantro, and chili peppers for added flavor and heat. The acidity of the citrus juice "cooks" the fish, giving it a firm texture and tangy flavor that is complemented by the aromatic herbs and spices. Ceviche is often served as an appetizer or light lunch, accompanied by crispy corn tortillas or toasted bread for scooping up the flavorful marinade. Variations of ceviche can be found throughout Chile, with regional ingredients and influences adding depth and complexity to this classic dish. Whether enjoyed on a sunny beachside terrace or at a bustling seafood market, sampling fresh ceviche is a culinary experience that captures the essence of Chile's coastal cuisine and the bounty of the Pacific Ocean.

- **Chilean Sea Bass:** Chilean sea bass, also known as Patagonian toothfish, is prized for its rich flavor, buttery texture, and versatility in cooking. This deep-sea fish is native to the cold, pristine waters of the Southern Ocean and is sustainably harvested off the coast of Chile. Chilean sea bass is renowned for its firm, white flesh and high oil content, which gives it a luscious mouthfeel and a distinctive flavor that is both delicate and robust. The fish can be prepared in a variety of ways, from simple pan-searing or grilling to more elaborate preparations such as poaching, steaming, or baking. Popular accompaniments for Chilean sea bass include citrus-infused sauces, herb-infused oils, and seasonal vegetables that complement the fish's natural flavors and textures. Whether served as a main course at a fine dining restaurant or as part of a casual seafood feast at home, Chilean sea bass is a true culinary indulgence that showcases the best of Chile's pristine waters and sustainable fishing practices.

- **Culinary Heritage:** Beyond their delicious flavors and textures, ceviche and Chilean sea bass hold a special place in Chile's culinary heritage, embodying the country's deep connection to the sea and its bounty. These iconic dishes have been enjoyed by generations of Chileans and have become an integral part of the country's cultural identity, celebrated in festivals, markets, and family gatherings throughout the year. Whether enjoyed as a simple street food snack or as part of an elaborate celebratory meal, ceviche and Chilean sea bass are symbols of Chile's maritime heritage and the enduring relationship between the people of Chile and the sea that sustains them.

In shorts, a seafood extravaganza in Chile is a feast for the senses, offering a tantalizing array of flavors, textures, and culinary delights that celebrate the country's rich maritime heritage and abundant natural resources. Whether sampling fresh ceviche on a sunny beach or savoring succulent Chilean sea bass at a waterfront restaurant, seafood lovers are sure to be enchanted by the vibrant flavors and culinary traditions of Chile's coastal cuisine. So come join us on a culinary journey to Chile's seafood paradise, where every bite is a celebration of the sea and the bounty it provides. Bon appétit!

CHAPTER SEVEN
MORE INSIDER TIPS AND BEYOND

In Chapter Seven, we delve deeper into Chile's hidden gems and insider secrets, providing readers with invaluable tips and recommendations to enhance their travel experience beyond the beaten path. From off-the-grid destinations to unique cultural experiences, this chapter offers a glimpse into the lesser-known aspects of Chile that are waiting to be discovered. Whether you're seeking adventure, relaxation, or cultural immersion, Chapter Seven is your guide to unlocking the secrets of Chile and creating memories that will last a lifetime.

Explore the remote villages of the Atacama Desert, where ancient traditions and breathtaking landscapes converge to offer a truly authentic Chilean experience. Discover the vibrant street art scene in Valparaíso, where colorful murals and graffiti adorn the city's hillsides and alleyways, telling stories of Chile's past and present. Venture off the beaten path to the mystical island of Chiloé, where centuries-old churches, traditional palafitos, and enchanting myths and legends await. With insider tips and hidden gems waiting to be uncovered, Chapter 7 invites readers to go beyond the guidebook and embrace the spirit of adventure as they journey through the diverse and enchanting landscapes of Chile.

HANGA ROA

ECO-FRIENDLY TRAVEL PRACTICES

As travelers increasingly seek environmentally responsible and socially conscious ways to explore the world, sustainable tourism has emerged as a critical focus for preserving natural landscapes, protecting cultural heritage, and supporting local communities. In Chile, a country blessed with stunning natural beauty and rich cultural diversity, eco-friendly travel practices play a vital role in ensuring the long-term sustainability of the tourism industry and the preservation of its unique ecosystems.

1. **Responsible Wildlife Viewing:** One of the cornerstones of eco-friendly travel in Chile is responsible wildlife viewing, which aims to minimize disturbance to natural habitats and respect the welfare of wildlife. When observing animals in their natural environment, it's important to keep a safe distance, avoid feeding or touching wild animals, and refrain from making loud noises or sudden movements that could cause stress or disruption. By following these guidelines, travelers can enjoy the beauty of Chile's diverse wildlife—from majestic condors soaring over the Andes to playful sea lions basking on rocky shores—while ensuring that their presence has minimal impact on the delicate balance of the ecosystem.

2. **Supporting Local Communities:** Another key aspect of sustainable tourism in Chile is supporting local communities and indigenous peoples who depend on tourism for their livelihoods. By patronizing locally owned businesses, staying in eco-friendly accommodations, and participating in community-based tourism initiatives, travelers can contribute directly to the economic empowerment and cultural preservation of local communities. From purchasing handmade crafts at artisan markets to enjoying homestay experiences with indigenous families, engaging with local communities offers travelers a deeper understanding of Chilean culture and traditions while fostering mutual respect and appreciation between visitors and hosts.

3. **Reducing Environmental Footprint:** In addition to supporting local communities, eco-friendly travel in Chile involves minimizing one's environmental footprint through conscious choices and responsible behavior. This includes reducing waste by using reusable water bottles, shopping bags, and toiletry containers; conserving energy by turning off lights and air conditioning when not in use; and opting for eco-friendly transportation options such as public transit, biking, or walking whenever possible. Travelers can also support conservation efforts by participating in volunteer activities such as beach

cleanups, tree planting initiatives, and wildlife monitoring programs, which help protect Chile's natural resources and promote environmental stewardship for future generations.

4. **Choosing Sustainable Accommodations:** When selecting accommodations in Chile, travelers can prioritize eco-friendly hotels, lodges, and eco-lodges that have implemented sustainable practices such as energy efficiency, waste reduction, water conservation, and support for local conservation projects. Many eco-friendly accommodations in Chile are certified by internationally recognized organizations such as EarthCheck, LEED, or Green Key, which verify their commitment to environmental sustainability and social responsibility. By staying at eco-friendly accommodations, travelers can enjoy a comfortable and responsible travel experience while supporting businesses that are dedicated to minimizing their environmental impact and preserving Chile's natural beauty for future generations.

5. **Promoting Sustainable Transportation:** Another important aspect of eco-friendly travel in Chile is promoting sustainable transportation options that reduce carbon emissions and minimize environmental impact. Travelers can opt for public transportation, such as buses or trains, which have

lower emissions per passenger compared to private vehicles. Additionally, many cities in Chile offer bike-sharing programs and have designated bike lanes, making cycling a convenient and eco-friendly way to explore urban areas while reducing traffic congestion and air pollution.

6. **Supporting Conservation Projects:** Travelers interested in eco-friendly travel can also support conservation projects and initiatives that protect Chile's natural habitats and biodiversity. Many organizations and non-profits in Chile work tirelessly to preserve endangered species, restore degraded ecosystems, and promote sustainable land management practices. By volunteering with conservation projects, donating to environmental organizations, or participating in eco-tours that support conservation efforts, travelers can make a meaningful contribution to preserving Chile's natural heritage and promoting sustainable tourism.

7. **Respecting Indigenous Rights and Cultural Heritage:** In addition to supporting environmental conservation, eco-friendly travel in Chile also involves respecting indigenous rights and cultural heritage. Many indigenous communities in Chile have a deep spiritual connection to the land and rely on traditional knowledge and practices for their livelihoods. Travelers can show respect for

indigenous cultures by seeking permission before entering indigenous territories, following cultural protocols and customs, and supporting indigenous-owned businesses and cooperatives. By fostering mutual respect and understanding between travelers and indigenous communities, eco-friendly travel can promote cultural preservation and empower indigenous peoples to protect their ancestral lands and traditions.

8. **Educating and Raising Awareness:** Education and awareness-raising are essential components of eco-friendly travel in Chile, as they help travelers understand the importance of sustainable tourism practices and their role in preserving the environment and supporting local communities. Tour operators, travel agencies, and government agencies can play a crucial role in educating travelers about eco-friendly travel options, promoting responsible tourism guidelines, and highlighting the benefits of sustainable tourism for both travelers and destinations. By raising awareness about environmental issues, promoting ethical tourism practices, and providing information about sustainable travel options, we can inspire travelers to make informed choices that minimize their environmental impact and maximize their positive contributions to Chile's sustainable tourism industry.

In a nutshell, eco-friendly travel practices are essential for promoting sustainable tourism in Chile and ensuring the long-term preservation of the country's natural beauty, cultural heritage, and biodiversity. By adopting eco-friendly transportation options, supporting conservation projects, respecting indigenous rights and cultural heritage, and raising awareness about sustainable tourism, travelers can make a positive impact on Chile's tourism industry while enjoying an enriching and authentic travel experience. Together, we can work towards a more sustainable and responsible approach to travel that benefits both travelers and the environment.

LAGUNA LEJÍA

HIDDEN GEMS AND OFF-THE-BEATEN-PATH DESTINATIONS

While Chile is renowned for its iconic attractions such as Torres del Paine National Park and Easter Island, the country is also home to a wealth of hidden gems and off-the-beaten-path destinations that offer unique experiences for adventurous travelers seeking to explore beyond the tourist trail. From remote wilderness areas and secluded beaches to quaint villages and ancient archaeological sites, Chile's hidden gems are waiting to be discovered by intrepid explorers looking to uncover the country's lesser-known treasures.

1. **Chiloé Archipelago:** One of Chile's best-kept secrets, the Chiloé Archipelago is a magical destination characterized by lush forests, rolling hills, and charming fishing villages. Located off the coast of southern Chile, Chiloé is known for its distinctive wooden churches, traditional palafitos (stilt houses), and vibrant folklore, including the myth of the Chilote ghost ship. Visitors to Chiloé can explore the island's rich cultural heritage by visiting UNESCO World Heritage-listed churches, sampling local dishes such as curanto (a traditional seafood stew cooked in an earth oven), and participating in traditional festivals and celebrations. Nature lovers will also find plenty to see and do in Chiloé, with

opportunities for hiking, birdwatching, and kayaking in the island's pristine natural reserves and coastal wetlands.

2. **San Pedro de Atacama:** Nestled in the heart of the Atacama Desert, San Pedro de Atacama is a hidden oasis that offers a stark contrast to the arid landscapes of the surrounding desert. This charming town is a haven for adventure seekers and nature enthusiasts, with a plethora of outdoor activities and attractions to explore. Visitors can embark on guided tours to explore otherworldly landscapes such as the Moon Valley, the Atacama Salt Flat, and the Tatio Geysers, where they can witness breathtaking sunrises and sunsets over the desert horizon. For those seeking cultural immersion, San Pedro de Atacama is also home to indigenous communities such as the Atacameño people, who have inhabited the region for thousands of years and continue to preserve their traditional way of life through music, dance, and artisanal crafts.

3. **Carretera Austral:** For travelers seeking a truly off-the-beaten-path adventure, the Carretera Austral offers a rugged and remote journey through some of Chile's most pristine and untouched landscapes. Stretching over 1,200 kilometers through the southern regions of Aysen and Los Lagos, this scenic highway winds its way through dense forests,

towering mountains, and glacial fjords, connecting isolated communities and hidden gems along the way. Highlights of the Carretera Austral include the Queulat National Park, with its dramatic hanging glacier and lush temperate rainforest; the marble caves of Puerto Río Tranquilo, sculpted by millennia of water erosion; and the remote village of Caleta Tortel, known for its unique stilted walkways and wooden boardwalks. Traveling the Carretera Austral is not for the faint of heart, but for those willing to venture off the beaten path, it offers a once-in-a-lifetime opportunity to experience the raw beauty and untamed wilderness of southern Chile.

4. **Isla Mocha**: Isla Mocha is a remote and enchanting island located off the coast of central Chile, accessible only by boat or small aircraft. With its pristine beaches, dense forests, and abundant wildlife, Isla Mocha is a paradise for nature lovers and outdoor enthusiasts seeking an off-the-grid escape. Visitors to the island can hike through lush rainforests teeming with endemic flora and fauna, explore secluded coves and hidden waterfalls, and relax on deserted beaches with stunning views of the Pacific Ocean. Isla Mocha is also a haven for birdwatchers, with opportunities to spot rare seabirds such as the Juan Fernández petrel and the white-throated storm petrel nesting on the island's cliffs.

For those seeking adventure, Isla Mocha offers world-class surfing, with legendary breaks such as La Puntilla and Punta Lavapie offering challenging waves for experienced surfers.

5. **Valle del Elqui:** Nestled in the foothills of the Andes Mountains in northern Chile, the Valle del Elqui is a hidden gem known for its stunning natural beauty, fertile valleys, and clear night skies. This picturesque region is famous for its production of pisco, Chile's national spirit, which is made from locally grown grapes and distilled in traditional artisanal distilleries known as pisco bodegas. Visitors to the Valle del Elqui can tour these bodegas, learn about the pisco-making process, and sample a variety of pisco-based cocktails and spirits. The valley is also a popular destination for stargazing, thanks to its clear, unpolluted skies and high altitude, which provide excellent conditions for observing the stars and planets. Several observatories in the Valle del Elqui offer guided tours and astronomical experiences, allowing visitors to marvel at the wonders of the cosmos while learning about the region's rich astronomical heritage.

6. **Juan Fernández Islands:** Located 670 kilometers off the coast of central Chile, the Juan Fernández Islands are a remote archipelago that offers a truly off-the-beaten-path escape for adventurous travelers.

Comprising three main islands—Robinson Crusoe, Alexander Selkirk, and Santa Clara—the Juan Fernández Islands are a UNESCO World Biosphere Reserve known for their unique ecosystems and endemic flora and fauna. Visitors to the islands can hike through lush forests, swim in crystal-clear waters, and explore hidden coves and secluded beaches. The islands are also home to a diverse array of wildlife, including the Juan Fernández fur seal, the Juan Fernández firecrown hummingbird, and the Juan Fernández lobster, all of which are found nowhere else on Earth. With limited infrastructure and few tourists, the Juan Fernández Islands offer a rare opportunity to experience pristine nature and unspoiled wilderness in one of the most remote corners of Chile.

In essence, Chile's hidden gems and off-the-beaten-path destinations offer a wealth of opportunities for adventurous travelers to explore the country's diverse landscapes, rich cultural heritage, and pristine natural beauty. From the remote wilderness of Isla Mocha to the fertile valleys of the Valle del Elqui and the pristine islands of the Juan Fernández archipelago, Chile's hidden gems promise unforgettable experiences and memories that will last a lifetime. So pack your sense of adventure, leave the tourist crowds behind, and set out to discover the hidden treasures that await you in the hidden corners of Chile.

PUERTO VARAS

PRACTICAL TIPS FOR NAVIGATING CHILE'S UNIQUE TERRAIN AND CLIMATE

Chile's diverse terrain and climate present travelers with a range of challenges and opportunities when exploring this beautiful country. From the arid deserts of the north to the icy fjords of the south, navigating Chile's unique landscape requires careful planning, preparation, and flexibility. Here are some practical tips to help travelers make the most of their journey through Chile's varied terrain and climate.

1. **Pack for All Seasons:** Chile's longitudinal stretch results in a wide range of climates, from the arid Atacama Desert in the north to the chilly fjords of Patagonia in the south. When packing for your trip, be sure to include clothing suitable for all seasons, including lightweight and breathable fabrics for hot and dry climates, as well as warm layers and waterproof gear for cold and wet conditions. It's also important to pack sturdy footwear, sunscreen, sunglasses, and a hat to protect against the intense sun in the desert regions, as well as insect repellent for areas with mosquitoes and other pests.

2. **Prepare for Altitude:** Many of Chile's most popular destinations, including the Atacama Desert, the Andean highlands, and the Lake District, are located at high altitudes, where the air is thin and oxygen

levels are lower. To prevent altitude sickness and acclimatize more easily, travelers should take their time adjusting to higher altitudes, drink plenty of water, avoid alcohol and caffeine, and consider taking altitude sickness medication if necessary. It's also advisable to plan for shorter hikes and activities at higher altitudes until your body has had time to adjust.

3. **Be Flexible with Itineraries:** Chile's diverse terrain and unpredictable weather patterns can make travel plans subject to change at a moment's notice. Be prepared to be flexible with your itinerary and adapt to changing conditions, especially when traveling to remote or isolated areas. Keep an eye on weather forecasts and road conditions, and have alternative plans in place in case of inclement weather or unforeseen circumstances. It's also a good idea to allow extra time for travel between destinations, as road conditions and travel times can vary significantly depending on the terrain and weather conditions.

4. **Stay Hydrated and Sun Safe:** Chile's dry climate and high altitude can lead to increased risk of dehydration and sunburn, especially in the desert regions of the north. Be sure to drink plenty of water, especially when hiking or engaging in outdoor activities, and carry a refillable water bottle to stay

hydrated throughout the day. Additionally, wear sunscreen with a high SPF rating, reapply regularly, and seek shade during the hottest part of the day to avoid sunburn and heat exhaustion.

5. **Respect Nature and Wildlife:** Chile's diverse ecosystems are home to a wide variety of flora and fauna, including many rare and endangered species. When exploring natural areas, be sure to follow Leave No Trace principles, stay on designated trails, and avoid disturbing wildlife or damaging fragile habitats. Respect any wildlife viewing guidelines and maintain a safe distance from animals to minimize stress and disruption. By respecting nature and wildlife, travelers can help preserve Chile's natural heritage for future generations to enjoy.

6. **Plan for Remote Travel:** Many of Chile's most spectacular destinations are located in remote or isolated areas with limited infrastructure and services. When planning your trip, be sure to research transportation options, accommodations, and dining options in advance, especially if traveling to more remote regions such as Patagonia or the Atacama Desert. Consider booking guided tours or excursions with local operators who are familiar with the area and can provide insight and assistance during your travels. Additionally, be prepared for limited access to amenities such as ATMs,

pharmacies, and medical facilities in remote areas, and carry any necessary medications, supplies, and emergency contact information with you at all times.

Navigating Chile's unique terrain and climate requires careful planning, preparation, and flexibility to ensure a safe and enjoyable travel experience. By packing for all seasons, preparing for altitude, being flexible with itineraries, staying hydrated and sun safe, respecting nature and wildlife, and planning for remote travel, travelers can make the most of their journey through Chile's diverse landscapes and cultural heritage. With proper preparation and a spirit of adventure, travelers can explore Chile's hidden treasures and natural wonders while embracing the challenges and opportunities that come with navigating its unique terrain and climate.

CONCLUSION

As we bring our journey through "**Chile Unveiled**" to a close, we are left with a profound sense of awe and appreciation for the myriad wonders that this extraordinary country has to offer. From the majestic peaks of the Andes to the pristine shores of the Pacific Ocean, Chile's diverse landscapes, rich cultural heritage, and warm hospitality have captured our hearts and imaginations, leaving an indelible mark on our souls.

Throughout the pages of this travel guide, we have embarked on a virtual odyssey through Chile's hidden gems, off-the-beaten-path destinations, and iconic landmarks, uncovering the secrets of this enchanting land and discovering the beauty and diversity that lie beyond the tourist trail. We have marveled at the fiery sunsets of the Atacama Desert, trekked through ancient forests in search of elusive wildlife, and savored the flavors of traditional cuisine in bustling marketplaces and quaint village cafes.

But beyond the breathtaking scenery and exhilarating adventures, it is the people of Chile who have truly touched our hearts and inspired us with their warmth, resilience, and joie de vivre. From the humble fishermen of Chiloé to the indigenous Mapuche communities of the Lake District, we have been welcomed with open arms and embraced as honored guests, invited to share in the rich tapestry of Chilean culture and tradition.

As we bid farewell to "**Chile Unveiled**," we do so with a sense of gratitude for the experiences shared, the memories made, and the lessons learned along the way. May this travel guide serve as a companion and inspiration for future journeys to **Chile**, encouraging travelers to venture off the beaten path, explore new horizons, and embrace the spirit of adventure that lies at the heart of this remarkable country.

To the esteemed buyer of "**Chile Unveiled**," we extend our deepest appreciation and heartfelt gratitude for embarking on this journey with us. Your decision to explore the wonders of **Chile** through the pages of this travel guide speaks volumes about your adventurous spirit, curiosity, and appreciation for the beauty of the world around us.

As you immerse yourself in the rich tapestry of Chilean culture, nature, and adventure, we hope that "**Chile Unveiled**" serves as your trusted companion and source of inspiration, guiding you on a transformative voyage through the hidden gems and off-the-beaten-path destinations that await you in this captivating country.

Made in the USA
Coppell, TX
09 December 2024